Retro Romance

Retro Romance

Classic Tips for
Today's Couple

Cheryl and Joe Homme

COLLECTORS PRESS

PORTLAND, OREGON

Book Design: Wade Daughtry, Collectors Press, Inc.
Editor: Perry Ahern

Library of Congress Cataloging-in-Publication Data

Homme, Cheryl, 1961-
  Retro romance : classic tips for today's couple / by Cheryl and Joe Homme -- 1st American ed.
     p. cm.
   ISBN 1-888054-80-8 (hardcover : alk. paper)
  1. Man-woman relationships. 2. Love. 3. Courtship. I. Homme, Joe, 1959- II. Title.
   HQ801.H733 2003
   306.7--dc21
                                    2003005948

Printed in Singapore

987654321

Contents

What's it All About?
Romance Defined 6

I Can See Clearly Now
Priorities 8

To Tell the Truth
Trust 12

Watson, Come Here, I Need You
Communication 16

R-E-S-P-E-C-T
Honoring Each Other 20

And Away We Go
Getting Started 24

From Here to Eternity
Everyday 28

I Started a Joke
Sense of Humor/Laughter 32

This Old House
The Home Environment 36

Ask Not What Your Spouse Can do for You,
But What You Can do for Your Spouse
Division of Labor 40

Teach Your Children Well
Modeling Romantic Behavior 44

The Kids are All Right
Baby-sitters 48

A Night at the Opera
Dates 52

What's Money Got to do With It?
Romantic "Investments" 58

Whatcha Got Cookin'?
Food 62

I'll Play for You
Romantic Singers 66

The Sound of Music
Classic Romance Songs 70

Moving Pictures
Romantic Films 74

Against All Odds
Celebrated Couples 78

Who Wrote the Book of Love?
Books 82

Sealed With a Kiss
Love Letters 86

Shop in the Name of Love
Gift-giving 90

Kisses Sweeter Than Wine
The Kiss 94

Ticket to Ride
Travel 98

Celebrate Good Times
Holidays and Special Occasions 102

We Can Work it Out
Tiffs 106

I'm a Believer
Faith Matters 110

Learning to Fly
Intellectual Growth 114

Some Assembly Required
Hobbies 118

An Eye on the Prize
Goal Setting 122

Now and Forever
The Wrap-up 126

Acknowledgments
127

What's it All About?

Romance Defined

Dictionary definitions for romance are woefully inadequate. Even love, a word far greater in complexity, is better defined. Romance has, of course, many connotations and differs dramatically in meaning from one person to the next. For our purposes, we will define romance as: *a learned behavior that expresses love and caring from one mate to another.* The basic elements of romance are the willing gift of time and service to one's mate, and the willing sacrifice of self-interest in those pursuits. In addition to time, service, and sacrifice, perhaps the greatest element of all is thoughtfulness. These components combine to cement the union and provide a shelter from the storm while deepening the value and joy of the relationship.

I Can See Clearly Now

Priorities

Everyone is busy. Sure, some are busier than others, but we are all operating at about capacity. Probably all of us can recall the days of courting and identify it as a quieter and simpler time, largely free of today's hectic pace. In reality, then it was a question of prioritizing time, just as it is today.

- For our national and personal economy, work and productivity are very important. But as meaningful as your career may be, it pales in comparison to the importance of your relationship. This is a simple truth that we all can recognize.

  - Making an effort to shift a portion of time from work to home is tricky, but worthwhile. Of course, an abrupt change in work habits could be alarming to management and co-workers. A gradual approach is often more acceptable. If you are in a leadership position, learn to delegate some of your duties. In any position, sharing your job skills and experience will allow for increased flexibility in your schedule.
  - It is sometimes wise to turn down overtime. The extra time you spend at home might be more valuable than the extra dollars you could earn.
  - Do you dwell on your work during your time off? Consciously work on devoting that energy to your mate — a truly valuable use of time.
  - Share with your partner your desire and plan to make increased time together a priority over work. His or her ideas and support will make the transition easier.

- After toiling all day at work, many people are in the habit of coming home and toiling there as well, often late into the evening. Take time to relax with your mate, perhaps in a pre-appointed location, such as lounging on the deck, stretching out on the bed, or sitting together at the dining room table. This time of "reconnecting" demonstrates that your relationship comes first.

• Weekends hold great potential for approaching tasks together. Instead of taking an individual approach to that which needs tending, discuss in advance what might be undertaken as a team. Take regular breaks to rest, reconnect, and evaluate your efforts. You'll both relish the pride of seeing what you can accomplish together.

• Of course any honest discussion of time and priorities begs the question: where do I belong on my own priority list? The answer may well be that those who place their relationship above their own interests may ultimately gain the most personal satisfaction.

True Romance

I just can't quite seem to get enough rest when left to my own devices. I always try to wring just a few more hours out of a day to the point where I'm always on the verge of physical exhaustion. It's terrible, and I can't seem to help myself; there just seems to be so much that needs doing. But my wife, bless her heart, is having none of that. She insists that I get to bed at a decent hour. She claims (or, I should say, asserts) that my life will be more fun and I will get more accomplished if I'm rested. She has made it her personal quest that I get the rest I need.

—Bob

To Tell the Truth

Trust

Without trust, there can be no romance. Every effort should be made to establish and maintain trust in the relationship. If for any reason trust has been interrupted, both partners must commit to regaining it.

- It begins with you. Be a trustworthy person for your mate. It is difficult to trust your spouse if you practice deceit yourself.

- Open up to your beloved, trusting that you can genuinely convey your true feelings, thoughts, and ideas. Encourage the same in return.

- When your partner shares personal thoughts and ideas with you, treat his or her feelings with gentleness and respect.

- Be reliable, dependable, and on time.

- Allow your partner the gift of time for self-fulfillment, trusting that his or her personal growth is also positive for your relationship.

- Accept an apology graciously. Forgive immediately and completely (no fair bringing it up again later). This takes practice. Allow time and opportunity for breaches of trust to be repaired.

True Romance

Recently while socializing with a group of friends, the men started joking about silly mistakes their wives had made. I knew my husband had plenty of fuel for a "Can You Top This" story, but to my great relief, he didn't join in the contest. It was such a good feeling to know I could trust my best friend not to try for laughs at my expense.

—Claire

Watson, Come Here, I Need You

Communication

Communication is generally accepted as one of the most important elements of a successful relationship. Certainly the cause of romance benefits directly from the development of communication skills by allowing us to convey appreciation, respect, encouragement, and love. These expressions may be transmitted in a variety of ways including: body language, in writing, and, of course, verbally.

- Everyone loves receiving mail. Yet in this age of e-mail, faxes, and cell phones, how often do you receive personal correspondences in your postal box? Take time to write your dear one a hand-written note, greeting card, or postcard. Put on a stamp, and send it through the good old-fashioned mail.

- If it is okay with your spouse's employer, email him or her a quick update on what is going on in your day. This is an easy way to stay in touch, and since it can be read at one's leisure, does not interrupt important business.

- Leave a short love note for your sweetheart, tucked in an unexpected place, such as a shirt pocket, briefcase, lunch, or purse. "Sticky notes" are great for leaving quick expressions of love on a bathroom mirror, computer screen, or steering wheel.

- Remember Matt Dillon and Miss Kitty in *Gunsmoke*? That popular television program featured the most subtle of romances. Yet the characters' subtleties were highly communicative. Try a warm look from across a crowded room, a blown kiss, loving smiles, knowing nods, timed winks, and flirtatious glances.

- Strong verbal cues demonstrate security in a relationship. As often as possible, tell your beloved that you want, need, and love them.

- Common politeness is often neglected in day-to-day interactions. Get back in the habit of using phrases like "please," "thank you," "you're welcome," and "excuse me."

- Get in the practice of noticing the little things. "Boy, that shower looks great; thanks for cleaning it." Timely compliments show that his or her efforts are not taken for granted.

- Compliment your partner at least as often as you did when you were dating.

- A brief phone call will also be valued before an important meeting or interview to offer encouragement and boost confidence.

- Upon returning home, meet at the door and greet each other pleasantly with "Good to see you," or "I thought about you a lot today." Wait to discuss the ills of your day until after you have both had some time to relax.

- At least once a week, as an after dinner treat, retire to your porch, patio, deck, or den to get reacquainted.

- Begin a disagreement with a hug and words of commitment, "First, remember that I love you. Now, let's talk about what is going on."

- Declarations such as "You were right," "I will always love you," "You amaze me," "You are so smart," "You are so sexy," "You are my best friend," "You are my favorite person," and "What a cool idea," need to be said on a regular basis.

- Sometimes the most powerful words you can say are simply "I'm sorry."

- Tell your spouse when he or she is doing things right: "I love it when you call me your bride," or "I appreciate the way you stuck up for me just now."

- Say only positive things about your partner to other people: "My husband is a great cook," or "My wife is so thoughtful."

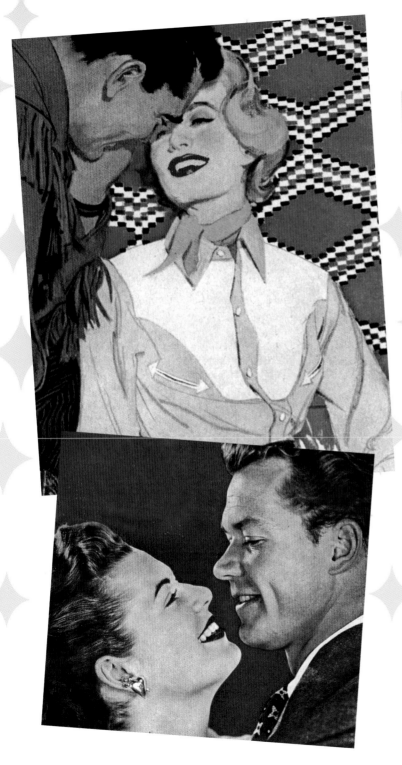

True Romance

One of the sweetest things my husband ever said to me came as a complete surprise and lightened an otherwise stressful situation. We awakened one morning to having no hot water. Great, so on Father's Day, yes, Father's Day, without the ability for anyone in the household to take a shower, there we were in the thick of it, trying to fix our hot water heater together. After much frustration trouble-shooting the cause of the problem, and with my temper rising, he turned to me and said, "There is no one I'd rather be doing this with than you." I immediately softened and reflected on this very romantic thing he had said, and I sighed and whispered, "Yes, I totally agree, if we have to struggle, I'd rather be right here with you — pulling together in the same direction."

—Audrey

R-E-S-P-E-C-T

Honoring Each Other

Over time, manners and courtliness can erode in a relationship. Frequently, a lack of manners and civility has more to do with life's frustrations than the relationship. Justification aside, harsh words, intemperate tones, and hostile body language convey a message of disrespect. It is a message that diminishes both parties, inflicting pain on the receiver and feelings of guilt on the sender. Couples need to be watchful that their manners, speech, and actions match the love and respect they feel for those who have so richly earned it.

- Polite terms such as "please" and "thank you" can almost always be expanded in their application.

- Displays of respect transfer easily to the relationship if they are well practiced outside of the relationship. Exhibit greater respect for friends, co-workers, and others.

- Show respect for your mate's friends too.

- There are gender-based jokes that are funny without humiliating the sex they lampoon. Avoid the retelling of those that overtly or subtlety convey disrespectful notions.

- Chivalry is not out of style:
    - If you are out of the habit of getting the door for your partner, renew your efforts in this area. This simple act of service is a highly demonstrative act of respect.
    - Dropping your spouse at the entrance and parking the car on your own is a courteous act, particularly on days of inclement weather.
    - Help her with her coat, pull out her chair, or extend an arm to help lead her through a dimly lit restaurant or theater.

- In social situations, see that your mate's needs are met before your own. Public displays of respect are uplifting.

- Listen to your partner, and respectfully acknowledge his or her thoughts.

- Show respect for your companion's role in the family. Regardless of how the labor is divided, display appreciation for each other. With this support, you give inspiration and courage to tackle each day.

True Romance

I think the main thing about romance is manners. We have chosen to be polite to each other in the smallest ways possible, as well as the biggest ways. The other day we were thinking about how much of the time in our twenty-nine year marriage we have actually been together. With remote work assignments, business and conference travel for both of us, I'm guessing that we have been physically together for twenty-seven and a half years. On every weekday of that entire time, my wife has made breakfast for me. I say for me, because I'm sure that she doesn't do it when I'm gone. Whatever the case, that's 7,170 breakfasts and second cups of coffee. I have done my very best to say "thank you" for every one of those cups of coffee. It's the right thing to do, when you think about it. If you are going to say "please" and "thank you" to strangers, it's a **must** to say it to the one you love most.

—Chet

And Away We Go

Getting Started

Most certainly, we are living in the information age. It is often said that information is power. So it is true in romance. Imagine the benefits of being "in the know" in the area of anniversaries, clothing sizes, and local events. Here's how to get started:

- Purchase a date book, appointment book, calendar, or use the "reminder" feature on your computer to keep track of important dates, including:

  - Your partner's birthday and all birthdays of friends and family that you observe.
  - Your wedding anniversary and those of close friends and family.
  - The anniversary of your first date, or other special event in your relationship.
  - School in-service dates (so you can plan trips out of town).
  - Annual medical check-up dates (so you can lovingly remind your spouse how important his or her health is to you).
  - It is perfectly acceptable to ask for help in compiling this information the first time. After that, it's up to you to keep the information current. The point here is not only to remember the dates that are traditionally celebrated, but also to be available to assist with party planning and gift buying.

- To demonstrate your commitment to participate in mutually important events, ask your mate to put a date/appointment book or calendar on your annual Christmas list.

• Have you ever found yourself traipsing around a store to find a person who is similar in size and body shape to your spouse and asking their size? Or showing a potential gift to a complete stranger and asking if they think your partner would like it? Avoid these ineffective techniques by recording the following "vital statistics" on a wallet-sized piece of paper:

For Her

Stocking Size
Hat Size
Sweater Size
Dress Size
Pants Size
Undergarment Sizes
Ring Size
Jacket Size
Hair Color
Eye Color
Favorite Clothing Line or Styles

For Him

Shirt Size
Pants Size
Shoe Size
Suit Size
Undergarment Sizes
Hat Size
Ring Size
Coat Size
Tie Preferences
Belt Size

You will need to have this information handy at all times, so have the paper laminated to prevent dog-earing in your wallet. Again, feel free to ask for assistance in compiling this information. Most are more than willing to share personal information to assist in proper gift selection.

True Romance

When Debbie and I first got together, there was never a lack of fun things to go out and do. But after children, careers, and a major family illness, we got out of the habit of going out. We found that our dating life needed a jumpstart. We decided the first thing we needed to do was get on some mailing lists. Now we are "in the know" about all sorts of community events, plays, and sporting events. We make a point of scanning the newspaper for fun attractions like concerts and comedy acts too. When the date opportunity arises, we are ready for it.

—John

From Here to Eternity

Everyday

Relationships have a common progression. Early on, the intensity of emotion is almost like a roller coaster ride. Later, this pace slows a bit as the partnership acclimates to everyday life. Sometimes we might look back at those early times with longing nostalgia, but maturity tells us that a certain degree of mellowing is more comfortable, and even necessary, to withstand the test of time. Another lesson provided through maturity is the ability to see the big picture and to recognize the beauty present in the everyday experiences shared with the person you love.

- Be noticeably grateful for having a partner with whom to share your life.

- When the alarm goes off in the morning, take a few minutes to snuggle before getting out of bed. This morning "connection" gets the day started in a more relaxed manner.

- Serve a cup of coffee with a kiss while he or she is getting ready for work.

- Keep your true love current on your whereabouts. It's nice to know you can easily reach each other in case of an emergency (or an urgent desire to express your love)!

- On the drive home from work, shift your mood from that of wage earner to that of a lucky person coming home to a loving spouse, happy children, and cozy home.

- When you arrive home, show your beloved as much attention as you do your children.

- After being away from each other, reconnect lovingly with warm expressions and by donning a pleasant demeanor — no matter how badly your day went. You can always discuss your day after you have shown some TLC.

- Seize opportunities for celebration. If one of you handled a situation with the children particularly well or felt especially motivated during a work assignment, there is reason enough for a toast during dinner!

- The frenzied pace of daily life should be slowed whenever possible. You can both help apply the brakes by not over scheduling your time with too many activities and commitments. A calm atmosphere is more conducive to romance.

- Spending time together each day is the best way to create opportunities for romance. Relax and hang out with each other.

- Many problems can be avoided with common courtesy. Treat the ones you love with more consideration than you would a casual acquaintance.

- Aim to have your words and actions correspond with each other. If you tell your darling that you will do something, willingly follow through.

- Make a meal for the family or vacuum the living room when it's not "your turn" or "your job."

- Those with mature relationships welcome quiet time. During times of silent togetherness, touch. Pat him as you walk by. Rub her feet while she is reading. Give him a light kiss on the cheek for no particular reason. Squeeze her hand.

- Kiss hello, goodbye, good morning, goodnight, and lots of times in between.

- Reflect daily on your love's best qualities. Ponder these attributes more than any negative traits he or she may have.

True Romance

My husband does so many sweet and thoughtful things that I am often accused of being spoiled. I know I can't deny it. When it's cold outside, he warms up the car, scrapes the windows, and drives up to the door for me. He offers me his coat when I'm chilly, even if I'm already dressed warmer than he is. He'll take me to a movie he doesn't really want to see, if he knows I'll like it. He fills my car with gas. After ordering at a restaurant, if his meal is more appealing than mine, he trades me. He's even willing to hold my purse while I go the restroom.

—Annie

I Started a Joke

Sense of Humor/Laughter

Laughter is a necessary part of life, and a sense of humor is key to keeping life in balance. The advantages of each do not end there. During courtship, these qualities are often equated with other positive attributes: humor with attractiveness, and laughter with contagious fun. The need for humor and laughter does not lessen in married life. In romantic relationships, its growth should be shared and continual.

- You already have the main ingredient for cultivating a sense of humor and making your own laughter and fun — each other. After all, what's more fun than being in love?

- Pick up a goofy desktop calendar that displays a new comic each day. Start the morning by sharing a bit of humor together.

- Laughter lets people "off the hook." If the two of you are in a tense conversation, try using humor to diffuse the situation. Good-natured laughter can melt away anxiety and be a true gift during a time of stress. If he or she blunders, calm the moment with humor. If you can train yourself to laugh at your own mistakes too, you'll be able to let *yourself* off the hook.

- Playful bantering can be a cherished part of your relationship. Loosen up a bit by incorporating some jesting or puns into your life. Joke around with each other using warm, sporting, and wholesome humor.

- Bring out the playful and humorous side of yourself. Encourage the same in your spouse. Tell your partner you like his or her sense of humor.

- A lot of jokes, humorous stories, and silly pictures are circulated via the Internet. Save the very best ones to share with each other.

- Watch TV and movie comedies together.

- Take in a comedic play or visit a comedy club.

- Save comic strips that mirror your lives in a humorous way.

- In social situations, use your sense of humor to keep the conversation upbeat and lively. Refrain from focusing on "shop talk," or gloomy news items. Discussing current events is important, but avoid concentrating on the horrific or negative aspects of the news.

- Each day brings new challenges. To take on life's unforeseen annoyances and "surprises" with humor and an even temper, discuss strategies for adopting a more optimistic outlook.

- Sometimes daily life can prove to be ridiculously absurd. View it as such, and rid yourselves of the frustrations. Suggest to your true love that you might have the makings for your own reality-based TV show!

True Romance

This is really embarrassing, but one cold fall morning I went out to start my husband's pickup so it would warm up a bit before he took off for work. I started the truck and went back inside. A few minutes later, as I was seeing him off at the door, I noticed that the truck was gone! In a near panic I said, "Somebody stole the truck." We live in a rural area, so there wasn't much chance of that, but how else would you explain this? My husband said, "Wait a minute, I think I hear it." Sure enough, it had rolled down the gradual slope of our driveway, then over a steep embankment causing it to "disappear." He tried to drive it out of the ditch, but it was too steep. We ended up calling a tow truck to get the pickup out of the ditch and my husband was late for work. All of this because I didn't set the parking brake. So, do you know what he said to me? Nothing. He just laughed. Not in a condescending way, but in a way that showed that he just wasn't going to take this situation seriously. I felt like such a fool, but he was so cool that it eased my embarrassment a little. Not only that, but as he was paying and chatting with the tow truck driver, he didn't let on that it was his wife who had lost the truck.

—Jeanette

This Old House

The Home Environment

Establishing a mood in the home that is conducive to comfort and relaxation complements romantic endeavors. A warm and peaceful home atmosphere allows a couple to escape the tensions of the outside world, while tending to each other's needs.

- Both partners should participate in decorating the home, so that the decor reflects each individual as well as the couple.

- Celebrate your marriage in your home decor, perhaps with photos of the two of you on vacation, your wedding certificate framed and hung in a prominent location, or the sheet music for "your song" in a picture frame.

- Adjustable dimmer switches allow for dial-a-mood lighting.

- Arrange home furnishings with an eye for relaxation, reduced maintenance, and space for leisure activities. For example, make living areas more open, reducing clutter and subconscious feelings of claustrophobia.

- An assortment of leafy or flowering plants will brighten up the home. This is especially helpful in northern regions with long winters and reduced sunlight.

- The mood and atmosphere in the home is primarily set by its occupants. Relax and speak in softer tones. Keep a ready smile on hand for the one you love.

- The home can be a sanctuary from outside interference. If the two of you would rather not take any phone calls, let the answering machine pick up, or unplug the phone altogether.

- Weekends are made for rest and recuperation. By all means, dress comfortably but spruce up enough to let your spouse know you care about your appearance in his or her presence.

- The home is a warmer place if all parties do their part to maintain it, so help around the house. Setting your sights on doing more than your share is very romantic.

True Romance

I make every effort to maintain an intimate ambiance in our bedroom. I try to keep dirty clothes, children's toys, stacks of paper, television noise, and lotion bottles and make-up jars from cluttering our sanctuary. The rest of the house might look like a daycare center at times, but our bedroom is clean, quiet, and romantic at the end of the day.

— Brenda

Ask Not What Your Spouse Can do for You, But What You Can do for Your Spouse

Division of Labor

Every marriage has its divisions of labor — the kind of labor directly associated with, and in support of, the family. The tasks involved are sometimes referred to as chores, and if they share any common components, it would be the repetitive nature and general lack of appreciation by others for their accomplishment. It's day-to-day stuff. In many families, the labor is divided largely along gender lines: a "man's job" and "woman's work." Increasingly, however, the lines have blurred — as well they should. The cause of romance, and the many gifts it bestows on a marriage, is furthered when labor conventions are ignored and both of you cooperatively serve the family and lighten each other's burdens.

- Undoubtedly, there are a number of chores that your partner takes care of altogether. Ask for a "training session" so that when the need arises, you can step in to help.

- There are a number of ways to assist your loved one:
  - Work alongside each other and share fellowship while a job is being accomplished.
  - Trade off chores on a weekly or monthly basis.
  - Volunteer to fully undertake a certain duty in order to free him or her up for some much-needed rest or a hobby.
  - Perform the work entirely on your own as a surprise.

- If you are not sure what needs to be done, ask.

- No matter how you choose to help, perform tasks cheerfully and without expectation of a return favor.

- Some chores cry out for professional services. Arrange for difficult or tedious domestic work, such as painting, carpet shampooing, or window washing, to be performed by others. A chore-oriented gift idea might include a weekend maid service to free both of you up for a special project or to simply go out and have some fun.

- Some unpleasant or messy chores may go undone. It's the odd job: the touch up painting, broken trim repair, or leaky faucet fix. Pick one and get the job done. Your mate will appreciate your efforts.

- So much joy is found in serving your companion that it might be hard to tell which of you benefits most. For this reason alone, there is no point in keeping a mental balance sheet of chores performed in competition with your spouse.

True Romance

How is my husband romantic? Well, I would say he's romantic because he gives me excellent backrubs, plus he does his own laundry.

— Julia

Teach Your Children Well

Modeling Romantic Behavior

Children bring considerable joy to a marriage. Although challenges lie ahead, parents look forward to raising their children, watching them grow in size and maturity. Sometimes it seems there is little time for the many lessons that need to be taught. Since time with the children at home is fleeting, we must prioritize our plans to maximize the fruits of our efforts. Generally, the basics and Golden Rule are covered as we try to prepare them to experience life on their own. It sounds simple enough, but it is no small task. One important area of learning, luckily, takes little time away from other lessons. Indeed, it is taught concurrently. That important lesson is how to achieve and maintain a strong, healthy, and romantic marriage. The resources for teaching this "class" are found in your own marital relationship.

- Show respect for each other in front of your children with kind words, a pleasant tone of voice, and warm body language. In modeling this behavior, your actions speak more convincingly than words.

- Set exemplary standards of commitment by being home on time, calling when you are running late, and helping with family matters.

- When appropriate, be demonstrative by holding hands, sitting close to each other, kissing each other good morning and good-bye. By observing this, children realize that it is okay for moms and dads to be affectionate.

- Let your children hear you say "I love you" to each other.

- Your kids will benefit from witnessing you enjoying each other's company. Let them see you smile and laugh. Let it be clear from words and actions that you like being together.

- Let your family members see you listening in a considerate manner when your partner speaks, so they understand that you value what he or she is saying.

- Have candid conversations with your children about the importance of relationships and what commitment means to the two of you.

- At age-appropriate times, openly discuss with your kids your vision on how a couple can balance a married life full of romance, children, and careers.

- Stand united with your spouse when discussing matters with your children. Work out your "game plan" ahead of time whenever possible.

- Sometimes a good parent becomes so focused on the children that a spouse is neglected. One of the best things you can do for your kids is to maintain a strong bond with your parenting partner.

- Make admiring statements about your partner in the presence of your kids. "Doesn't your dad look great?" or "Can you believe what a wonderful cook your mom is?"

- When alone with your kids, continue to speak well of your spouse. "I can't wait for your dad to get home — he's so much fun!" or "I sure love your mother — what a great lady."

- The children must understand that respect for your spouse is mandatory. Lead by example.

- Demonstrate a team approach by reminding your children you need to discuss important matters with your spouse before making a decision. "Your mom and I will discuss it and let you know."

- If your children see you having a disagreement, make sure they also see that you have made up. They need to understand that people can get angry, but still love and respect each other.

- When your family experiences difficult times, reaffirm the importance of relationships by expressing the value of still "having each other."

Children learn from all that you do and say, and from all that you leave undone and unsaid. As parents, you are always teaching, even when you think your kids are not paying attention. Someday, your children will be raising your grandchildren. Visualize how your own marital behaviors might influence this process. Keep this in mind by raising your children and treating your spouse in a way you would like patterned in the future.

True Romance

I always try to make sure I take the kids to the flower shop with me to pick out flowers for my wife on Mother's Day. My wife also has the kids help choose my Father's Day cards. My wife and I are both teaching our children, in unstated ways, how to show love and kindness.

— Walt

The Kids are All Right

Baby-sitters

The well-being and security of children ranks utmost in parents' minds. Parents often feel a conflict between their desire for romance and dating, and feelings of guilt in leaving the children at home. This anxiety is greatly eased by dependable and trustworthy baby-sitter contacts. The confidence you'll feel when you have taken the steps to employ responsible caregivers will enable you to enjoy going out for relaxing dates, knowing that your kids are all right.

- When seeking baby-sitters, both parents should obtain referrals from friends, relatives, and neighbors.

- Young people interested in baby-sitting opportunities may also be contacted through clubs, churches, or service organizations.

- Interview baby-sitters you would like to add to your "on call" list. In the interview, you or your spouse might ask:
  - What is your age?
  - Tell me about your experience.
  - Which days and times are you available?
  - Do you have references?
  - Do you consider yourself responsible?
  - Have you taken a baby-sitting course?

- Before a new baby-sitter's first assignment, invite him or her over for a short, paid training session.
  - Familiarize him or her with your home and note any rooms that are off limits to your children. If you have a baby or a toddler, point out stairways, bathrooms, or other places of potential danger.
  - Discuss all safety procedures, including the location of fire escapes, first aid kits, and flashlights.
  - Discuss household rules and expectations (for both the care-giver and the children) including having friends over or talking on the phone.
  - Instruct the baby-sitter that your children must not be left unattended — even for a moment.

- Ask the sitter not to bring movies or video games for your children and not to watch television while the kids are awake, unless you have approved the selections.
- Discuss how you want discipline handled, and tell the baby-sitter about any special needs or concerns related to your child including any allergies.

• Before you leave the house with a baby-sitter in charge:
  - Write down the phone numbers where you can be contacted, and add the numbers of neighbors or family members in case you can't be reached including a list of emergency telephone numbers (police, fire, poison control, doctor, and hospital).
  - Tell the baby-sitter how to handle unexpected visitors and incoming phone calls. Leave a notepad and pen by the phone for messages.
  - Show the baby-sitter the meals or snacks you have planned for the kids.
  - Encourage the sitter to read to and play with the kids.
  - If desired, have two rented videos available so the children will have a choice of which movie to watch.
  - Explain bedtime procedures.
  - Before leaving, have the baby-sitter summarize what to do in case of an emergency.
  - Always leave the house while your child is awake.

• Trustworthy baby-sitters are incredibly valuable. Once you have established a list, keep it current, so you'll have several you can call.

• Baby-sitters are more likely to be available when you are known to be a generous client, so pay them well.

True Romance

I appreciate that when my husband plans a date for my birthday or other special occasion, he also takes care of contacting a baby-sitter. All I have to do is get dressed!

— **May**

A Night at the Opera

Dates

For most people, the art of romance was first learned via the dating ritual. In the beginning we were awkward and more than a little nervous, and it seemed that just getting through the date without uttering something regretful was enough. Thankfully, we matured and eventually, through dating, we found someone we liked and trusted who became our best friend and with whom we fell in love. It was dating that allowed us to display love and commitment while having fun. Dating was, and is, at the heart of romance. So why would we ever want it to end?

- During courtship, dates were *requested*. Hearken back to those times and formally ask your love for a date. This can be done by phone, in person, or more elaborately by a written, mailed invitation.

- When planning a date, be sure to take care of all the details: arrange a baby-sitter, write down contact numbers, make reservations, and fill the car with gas. Neither of you will have a thing to worry about!

- Several other tasks can be performed in advance of a date that will contribute to its success. For example, when planning to take in a movie, pre-purchase tickets to avoid standing in line with your date. If a late night is planned, invite your spouse to take a nap so that he or she might feel well rested for the evening's festivities. For an outdoor date, remember to bring sun protection or insect repellant. Think ahead to what will make your time together more comfortable and enjoyable.

- We often overlook local events and attractions and wait for outside talent to arrive, yet every community has its own skilled and practiced entertainers. How romantic for you and your mate to undertake the process of discovery in seeking out talent and events that are just right for the two of you.

- Remember, others travel hundreds of miles to experience scenic or historic attractions in your own area. Take time to enjoy your local museums, state parks, and other "tourist attractions" together.

- Plan a picnic lunch or dinner at a scenic location. Spread out a blanket, or bring lawn chairs and a card table to get the meal "off the ground." The menu is open to creativity.

- Theme dates, whether serious or seriously goofy, can be an enjoyable change of pace. For example, a faux French foray might include a meal of a French dip with French fries followed by French vanilla ice cream for dessert. Then you might whisk your date home for a romantic faux French film like the Peter Sellers Inspector Clouseau classic, *A Shot in the Dark*. This is an area where your imagination can run wild.

- Find a co-conspirator for an extra special surprise. While dining at a favorite restaurant, have the waiter bring your date a bouquet of flowers or a gift that you delivered before the two of you arrived. The surprise will be complete.

- An *at home* date can be fun and budget-friendly. Send the kids out with a baby-sitter or put them to bed early. Prepare a romantic meal of fondue, for example. Get out a tablecloth and your best dishes. Remember the candles!

- During courtship, thank-yous are usually exchanged for a date. Extend this courtesy to your partner. Your "thank you for the date" can be expressed in person, over the phone, or more formally in a hand-written note.

If it's been a while since you and your spouse have dated, have realistic expectations. The lifestyle and schedule to which you have grown accustomed may have slowly edged out dating. Now is the right time to reintroduce it. With regular use, dating is a wonderful tonic for the married couple.

True Romance

We both don "professional" attire for the workplace. My wife's appearance is appropriate for work, and the same clothes, in my opinion, would be fine for when we go out. That's not the way she sees it, though. She thinks that I deserve better, so she dresses accordingly. That is not to say she maintains a vast wardrobe — it's just that she wants me to know that for her there is a real distinction between her work and personal life.

— Dan

What's Money Got to do With It?

Romantic "Investments"

It seems everything in life would be easier, and the outcome better, if there were a few more dollars to spend. Retailers espouse a similar sentiment with a spin: if you own our product, your life will be better. The message is that money or material wealth are effective lubricants, allowing a person to slip past many of life's difficulties and inconveniences. Like it or not, there is truth to that premise. But it is a limited truth. Thankfully, the things that matter most are not dependent on personal wealth. Simply put, love cannot be purchased and romance isn't for sale. In fact, the expression of love through time, service, sacrifice, and thoughtfulness is best practiced — and more meaningful to the recipient — if the financial outlay is kept to a minimum.

- Make a light snack — something as simple as cheese and crackers perhaps. Put on the music you fell in love to. Dust off those family photo albums and spend some time together on the couch pouring over memories.

- When it comes to romantic gift-giving, a handcrafted item trumps any gift you can buy — every time. If you are not particularly artistic or inventive, perhaps you just haven't found a medium in which you can comfortably express yourself. The key is to be realistic. If you are not handy with power tools, building a gazebo as a first project may not be a good choice. Use your creativity to discover what you can do. No matter how simple or elaborate, in each handmade gift there is a giving of yourself to the one you love.

- Remember the Ventures' tune, "Walk Don't Run"? It seems they were really on to something. Walking provides stress-relieving exercise that is relatively easy on muscles and joints, making it a sustainable form of low-impact athletic activity. Walking is well suited for romance as well. Whether your pace is fast or leisurely, there is ample time, and breath, for conversation. Like most things romantic, the possibilities are endless. You might go for a walk every night at a pre-appointed time, or you might fit it in when you can. You might hold hands. You might power walk. One thing is for sure — walking is a unique opportunity for a couple to talk, relax, and reduce stress while exercising. You may find that your walks get longer and longer all the time — both because you are getting in better shape, and because you enjoy it so much.

- Perhaps the ultimate in pampering is the spa weekend. These getaways have long been touted as the best in relaxation and body care. Much of the allure of the spa is the degree of personal service. Most have a competent and professional staff to cater to your needs, which definitely adds to the experience. But imagine the benefits of a spa owned and operated by the most trusted person in your life — your spouse. That would be the ultimate in care and relaxation. It is possible to have this experience right in your own home. It will take a bit of creativity and a little research, but will pay off big in romance dividends because your efforts will show. Here's how:
  - Start at a hair salon and ask for help. Tell them you are looking for hair and skin products to incorporate into a pampered spouse package. Ask how the products are used and their benefits. These "co-conspirators" will be happy to give you an overview on how to give a facial or manicure.
  - Stop by the grocery store to buy a beverage and a light snack you can prepare.
  - Next, begin setting up the spa environment. (Nothing over the top mind you. After all, the emphasis is on personal service.) If childcare is needed, see to it. Turn off the phone and tune in relaxing music. Put the lights down low and you're ready to begin.
  - Give a facial, shampoo, massage, and apply skin moisturizer, if desired. The cause of romance will be served through your time and effort.

- If your companion has a long drive ahead or a daily commute, consider ways to make the trip more comfortable, such as compiling a cassette or compact disc of favorite songs. This will help reduce the stress of traveling and may keep him or her more alert on the road.

- When the weather outside is frightful, and the sheets on your bed are icy cold too, jump in on your spouse's side and warm the sheets with your body heat. When your spouse comes to bed, move over to your own side. Sheet warming, along with allowing your spouse to warm his or her feet on your bare legs, will be viewed as an unparalleled act of romantic heroism.

- Romance can be as simple as drawing a bath for each other. Top it off by warming a towel or pajamas in the dryer.

True Romance

Joe decided to create a very special Christmas gift for me one year. He asked our sons, then ages 4 and 10, "Why is mom a good mom?" and wrote down their exact responses. He transcribed their replies and the boys illustrated them. Here is what our 4-year-old said, verbatim: "Why Mom Is Such a Good Mom? Because I love her so much, I just love her. I love her because I like her. She gives me food. She plays with me a lot. She does things to make me happy." This simple item is one of the greatest gifts I've ever been given, and I'll treasure it always.

—Cheryl

Whatcha Got Cookin'?

Food

Few romantic images are more powerful than a candle-light dinner at a quiet table for two. Dining and romance are quite naturally viewed in tandem, and for good reason — dinner dates bring couples face-to-face, stimulating lively discourse and intimacy through eye contact. It is as potent a tool for interaction in a long-term relationship as it was in early dating.

- Some couples feel that breakfast in bed is one of the most romantic ways to start the day. It's the gesture that counts — surprise your spouse with a simple breakfast of toasted English muffins, strawberries, a glass of fruit juice, and a cup of coffee or tea.

- On a weekend, whisk your partner away for a romantic breakfast.

- Although extravagant cuisine isn't standard fare for most couples, on special occasions try serving foods that conjure up romance, such as lobster, oysters, or filet mignon. Or, as an indulgence some evening, sample a small jar of caviar served with crackers and creamed cheese. Top if off with mousse or a fabulous chocolate dessert as another grand gesture!

- If you are not the principal chef in your family, surprise him or her by helping with the meal, setting the table, or volunteering to prepare a side dish or salad.

- If the primary cook in your family has had a difficult or extra busy week, arrange to bring dinner home with you, have it delivered, or call ahead to announce that the two of you are going out!

- Dress up your table for a romantic dinner. Use a centerpiece, tablecloth, candles, and your best dishes. Tune in some soft background music.

- If you're both particularly fond of a certain ethnic cuisine, enroll in a cooking class together or buy a cookbook to learn how to prepare some new and exciting meals at home.

- When making reservations for a birthday or anniversary celebration, be sure to let your host or hostess know it's a special day. Often, restaurants will give you VIP treatment, including a better table or special dessert.

- Picnics are back in style! With fresh air and fewer distractions, picnics are a fun, relaxing, and romantic ways to share a meal. Be spontaneous, or buy a fully equipped picnic basket. Menu suggestions:
  - Traditional – sandwiches or fried chicken with chips and cookies.
  - Romantic – cheese, crackers, strawberries, chocolates, and wine.
  - Creative – anything that will be special or meaningful to your date.
  - Gather wildflowers for a "centerpiece." Lie on a blanket and look at cloud shapes.

- For a "retro meal," go to a diner that has individual jukeboxes in the booths and order one beverage (and two straws) with a plate of fries to share.

- Buy a small appliance for the two of you to learn how to use together such as a waffle iron or fondue set. Laugh at your mistakes!

- Many other appealing foods, beverages, and sweets can be given as a "stocking stuffer" or as a romantic gift:
  - Gourmet coffees, flavored hot or iced teas
  - French or Swiss chocolates
  - Pie or pastry
  - Basket of exotic fruits
  - Assortment of imported cheeses
  - Pasta, breads, soups, or sauces
  - Fresh cherries
  - Gourmet herbs and spices

If you're like most people, you've become accustomed to doing many things in a rush, including eating. Slowing down the pace aids digestion and allows for more enjoyment of the food and conversation.

True Romance

My husband and I are often so busy it seems we hardly get a chance to speak with each other for days. One afternoon I called him at work to tell him I had to work late. He arranged to get off work a little early that day, stopped by the store, and came home to prepare my favorite meal of chicken enchiladas. He put the kids to bed a little early and by the time I arrived home, the mood was set. I was so surprised to come home to a candlelit table, rather than what I had expected — to come home to having to put together a meal in a rush. I was so appreciative of this unexpected special time together.

— Suzie

I'll Play for You

Romantic Singers

Singers and songwriters have long helped identify and define the feelings associated with love and romance. These artists have also been a source of inspiration for lovers. Romantic songs are a staple of many types of music, including jazz, country, soul, and rock. While the style and approach may differ, romantic songs of different genres have similarities in delivery. They tend to be sung with smooth, clear, and warm intonations. Even the most raucous singers will alter their approach to capture romance in song. It is important work — for couples have always been, and will always be, in need of music to fall in love to over and over again.

Crooners understand romance. From the big band sounds of the 1940s to today's Latin inspired music, crooners lay down tracks that are well produced and feature excellent musicians on songs that are disarmingly romantic.

- Frank Sinatra: Who else? Sinatra virtually invented vocal phrasing in modern music. From his subtle vocal style came a depth of emotion that seemed, at times, to divulge even more than he cared to express. Recommended Album: *Sinatra Reprise The Very Good Years*. Recommended Song: "Nancy."

- Nat King Cole: His style is smooth, warm, and personal. A tremendously popular artist for Capital Records who was obviously offered top-notch material, he always made the most of it and never failed to please. Recommended Album: *The Unforgettable Nat King Cole*. Recommended Song: "Unforgettable."

- Tony Bennett: A true original with a hip, engaging style. The hallmarks of his long career are continued artistic growth and passion; he loves his work. Recommended Album: *Tony Bennett Collection*. Recommended Song: "The Shadow of Your Smile."

Additional selections...

- Johnny Mathis: Recommended Album: *Johnny Mathis: 30 Favorites*. Recommended Song: "Chances Are."

- Matt Monro: Recommended Album: *20 Great Love Songs*. Recommended Song: "Somewhere."

- Dean Martin: Recommended Album: *The Best of Dean Martin 1962-1968*. Recommended Song: "In The Chapel In The Moonlight."

A number of artists who are less likely to be associated with romantic music have made substantial contributions to the field as well:

- Elvis Presley: His romantic renditions have an almost haunting quality, as if the singer is expressing feelings that are difficult, but necessary, to share. More than a touch of loneliness can be heard in that great voice, even when singing the joys of love. With his swagger and macho persona, Elvis, perhaps more than any other performer, proved once and for all that real men are romantic. Recommended Album: *The Elvis Presley Collection of Love Songs*. Recommended Song: "Loving You."

- The Beatles: In their relatively short career, the Beatles' musical output was enormous. A substantial amount of their catalog was devoted to romantic expression — music that is clever, thoughtful, and brimming with enthusiasm for that which matters most. Recommended Album: *The Beatles Love Songs*. Recommended Song: "Here, There And Everywhere."

Additional selections...

- The Platters: Recommended Album: *The Very Best of the Platters*. Recommended Song: "Twilight Time."

- Marvin Gaye: Recommended Album: *Marvin Gaye Anthology*. Recommended Song: "Ain't No Mountain High Enough."

- The Everly Brothers: Recommended Album: *The Very Best of the Everly Brothers*. Recommended Song: "Let It Be Me."

- The Beach Boys: Recommended Album: *Pet Sounds*. Recommended Song: "God Only Knows."

To be an active romantic, listen for and seek out artists the two of you can share when the hi-fi is high and the lights are down low.

True Romance

Some music actually seems to be able to enhance our collective mood. My wife and I, when we want to really relax, unwind, and mellow out, tune in the radio station that plays standards of the 40s & 50s. Although we did not grow up in this era, we find the soothing effects of singers like Sinatra and Bennett make for great background music while still being able to maintain a conversation.

— Dave

The Sound of Music

Classic Romance Songs

To develop a list of some of the greatest romantic songs ever recorded, we must consider what makes a romantic song great. Effective romantic songs have a memorable melody that is appropriate to the subject matter. The singer sincerely conveys the feeling of love. But most important are the words. The lyrics might relate the joy of newfound love or its enduring quality. They might express the value of love or try to define the feeling of love. Whatever the approach, the words must communicate sufficient warmth, truth, and understanding that listeners feel the song is speaking for them.

Selected romantic classics:

- "In My Life" by The Beatles: In this song, John Lennon and Paul McCartney recall friends and places from their past while lamenting the changes brought on by time. From these recollections, perspective for the present and future is gained, leading to a clarification and affirmation of the loved one's place in the singer's heart. The subject matter is of great emotional complexity, but the presentation is basic and pure, making it the stuff of classics.

- "Love is a Many Splendored Thing" by The Four Aces, The Ames Brothers, and Peter & Gordon: A wide variety of artists and groups have recorded this one, and for good reason — it is a great song. In a host of metaphors, the listener is swept away on a visual tour to explain the meaning of love. The song culminates with a sudden personal statement that brings the listener back to reality. It seems that the statement has come out of nowhere, but upon reflection, its origins are plain — for it comes straight from the heart.

- "Stand By Me" by Ben E. King: This is a song stripped of all pretenses with an open display of vulnerability. The song opens as night is settling upon the land. The singer states that the encroaching darkness won't make him fearful if his true love will stand at his side. He doesn't stop there. Soon he describes all manner of natural disasters, explaining that he won't fear those events either if she stands by his side. This is an awesome emotional declaration evidenced by the singer's willingness to share his fears and bare his soul for the one he loves.

- "Longer" by Dan Fogelberg: "Longer" is a song about a relationship examined over time. Beginning with the past, the singer states that he always loved his partner. In the present, the message is the same — love has endured. For the future, come what may, the pledge is renewed for an everlasting love. It is a song that states what the romantic in all of us knows: the gift of love is not time sensitive. Indeed, it tends to grow as time goes by.

Additional selections...

- "Devoted To You" by The Everly Brothers
- "The Very Thought of You" by Nat King Cole
- "Fly Me To The Moon" by Frank Sinatra
- "Things We Said Today" by The Beatles
- "Unchained Melody" by The Righteous Brothers
- "You Send Me" by Sam Cooke
- "I Want You, I Need You, I Love You" by Elvis Presley
- "It Takes Two" by Marvin Gaye & Kim Weston
- "Maybe I'm Amazed" by Paul McCartney
- "I Can't Help Falling In Love" by Elvis Presley
- "You Make Me Feel Brand New" by The Stylistics
- "I Love How You Love Me" by Bobby Vinton
- "Something" by The Beatles
- "Love Me Tender" by Elvis Presley
- "Through The Years" by Kenny Rogers
- "How Sweet It Is To Be Loved By You"
  by Marvin Gaye

This is but a sampling. Many more songs could
be considered romantic classics. Certainly any
song deemed by the two of you as "our song"
will always be regarded as one of the greatest.

True Romance

First of all, I want to make it clear that my husband is *not* a fan of disco music. Anyone who knows him would attest to that. Now that that's out of the way, let me tell you about "our song." We both attended the same high school, but didn't really know each other very well. Unbeknownst to me, he had his eye on me and, secretly, I thought he was kind of cute. Anyway, I was chatting with a couple of girlfriends at a homecoming dance when he got up the courage to ask me to dance. Just as I agreed to dance with him, the band announced they were taking a break. That was a little awkward at first because we were just standing there. He really didn't have anything prepared to say because he assumed we would be dancing. But it was okay, because he made a joke out the awkwardness of the situation which I found charming. Anyway, the band starts up again and the first song they play isn't the Eagles, isn't Kansas, but a version of the Trammp's "Disco Inferno." This look came over his face that was priceless and it seemed to say, "Why did it have to be *this* song?" I tried to give him a way out, but he said that it was okay, the song didn't really matter — he just wanted to dance with me. (Such a charmer.) So we danced to the song and that was the beginning of our life together. Because of that, "Disco Inferno" is "our song." On occasion one of us will put it on the CD player (yes, we bought it), and we dance to the music. It seems that we didn't chose our song, but that our song chose us.

—Jill

Moving Pictures

Romantic Films

Romantic films, as a genre, seem to defy description. There are a few standard plot lines, but to define a picture as romantic based on those is far too limiting. In the best romantic movies, there exists so many special moments of dialogue, character development, and superb acting, that there seems to be a message present for each viewer — a personal message from the filmmakers to the audience, an audience that understands human nature and the subject matter — an audience comprised of lovers.

Selected romantic movies:

- *The Last of the Mohicans:* Depending on your viewpoint, this might be a magnificent romantic film or an action/adventure movie. In reality, it is both. Set in the time of the French and Indian War, it takes place in what is to become New York State in that region's frontier days. In the beginning, the subject matter is broad: warring governments, issues of encroaching civilization on nature, and the impact of westward expansion on the indigenous peoples. Gradually, the story comes to focus on the love that develops between the characters Hawkeye and Cora. For all its action sequences, *The Last of the Mohicans* is — at heart — a story of service, devotion, and self-lessness.

- *Beauty and the Beast:* Here is a wonderfully entertaining and romantic movie. A film filled with music, comedy, and a great deal more. The story concerns Belle and the Beast, incarcerated together in a fantastic gothic mansion. She is serving a sentence of self-sacrifice. The Beast is imprisoned by his grotesque appearance, a consequence of his past sins. He can be freed from this punishment only by winning the heart of another. That, however, would seem impossible, for he is fully aware of his appearance, and the shame he feels for his past transgressions has turned from guilt to bitterness and self-loathing. For love, he knows that he has little to offer. He is utterly without hope. The movie speaks of the redeeming powers of love and the yielding of self-interest. The Beast learns that in love, all things are possible, and we can't help but be reminded of that fact for our own lives as well.

- *Casablanca:* A terrific cast, a film shot in dramatic black-and-white, and a backdrop of international intrigue are all components of this movie classic. Humphrey Bogart as Rick is a tough guy whose code is he "won't stick out his neck for nobody." Rick is reunited with his old flame, Ilsa, the object of his broken heart. But are they really reunited? The storyline concerns lost love and the costs associated with regaining it. It is about a higher calling and a sacrifice made for love.

- *Groundhog Day*: An original comedy that is strikingly romantic and poignant. The story concerns an acutely arrogant and egotistical TV weatherman who is forced into doing a remote broadcast from Punxsutawney, Pennsylvania, on Groundhog Day. He is above this sort of corny show and lets his staff know it — repeatedly. Once the program is finished, the team attempts to return home only to be turned back by inclement weather. They are all required to stay overnight in Punxsutawney. The next morning, the weatherman awakens to an exact replay of the previous day. It slowly dawns on him that everything is the same as the day before, but he is the only one who realizes it. The townspeople and his staff are completely oblivious to what is going on. It keeps happening day after day. His first inclination is to manipulate the phenomenon to his advantage. This cynical approach is the same one he has taken throughout his life, and in due time he finds his existence empty and meaningless. Slowly he learns — really learns — how to feel and care about others. This is when the movie is cleverly reshaped from comedic to the romantic.

- *West Side Story*: A retelling of *Romeo and Juliet* with plenty of classic songs and outstanding dance sequences. Tony and Maria find love in the most improbable surroundings, amidst the concrete, steel, and graffiti of the city where gangs rule and violence is a way of life. Theirs is a love that isn't supposed to happen; each has close ties to opposing ethnic gangs on the verge of warfare. These conflicts would seem insurmountable to anyone who wasn't in love, but for Tony and Maria the future holds nothing but hope. It's an emotionally complex and passionate film that well expresses the simple notion that love can never die.

Obviously, this list is only a sampling of romantic movies. Many more await discovery by you and your partner.

True Romance

I wouldn't say that my husband's taste in movies runs to the romantic. But I'll tell you this, he can be moved by a movie. We went to see *Field of Dreams* when it came out and it touched him in so many ways. First, he loves baseball, so there was that. But there was also a lot concerning the relationship between fathers and sons. Since he is a father and a son, that subject is near and dear to his heart too. And of course, there is the wife who stands by her husband's side through thick and thin — that kind of gets him too. I find it romantic that he so openly shares his emotions after seeing a movie like that. So, for us, a romantic movie is not what you might think of as your typical romantic movie.

—Kelli

Against All Odds

Celebrated Couples

Maintaining a healthy, happy marriage can be a challenge at any social or economic level. Perhaps the most challenging relationships are those conducted under the spotlight of the press, open to scrutiny by the masses. Celebrity marriages suffer from a lack of privacy, which is essential to working through the difficult times encountered in all relationships. Additional challenges include long separations due to work obligations, oversized egos, and other distractions that are out of proportion to ordinary life. Perhaps that is why, enduring celebrity relationships seem particularly noteworthy.

- George Burns & Gracie Allen: A personal and professional relationship that endured, in show business terms, from vaudeville to the age of television. Burns, at every opportunity, credited his wife for the success of their careers and their marriage. It was a shared adoration.

- Paul & Linda McCartney: If show business in general has inherent challenges for a relationship, what of those involving the world of rock-n-roll? For Paul and Linda it seemed to be a question of priorities. Through the trials of the Beatles breakup, to the overwhelming success of Wings and beyond, the pair was inseparable.

- James & Gloria Stewart: Married relatively late in life, this was a tremendously compatible couple whose devotion to each other was apparent to all who knew them.

- Ronald & Nancy Reagan: It is hard to imagine a more intense spotlight than the Presidency. This couple helped to weather the storm by serving as each other's biggest booster and greatest protector.

- Edward, Duke of Windsor & Wallis Warfield Simpson: What could possibly be more romantic than giving up a Kingship for the one you love?

- Abraham & Mary Todd Lincoln: In perhaps the world's most stressful job, during unquestionably the most harrowing of times in the nation's history, the Lincoln's marriage prevailed through national and personal tragedy. It was not an easy journey, publicly or privately, but this couple's devotion to each other in the face of adversity and the strength they would each draw from that devotion, is evidence of the gifts of marriage.

BACK HOME
FOR KEEPS

True Romance

My wife and I have marriage role models. It may seem kind of funny, since you don't really know what's going on in other couples' lives, but all the same, there is something really admirable about enduring relationships. We notice couples locally and even nationally who have withstood the test of time together, and from their example we know we can do the same.

—Doug

Who Wrote the Book of Love?

Books

To share your thoughts and opinions concerning reading material is to share something of yourself. Your choice in books and periodicals is often deeply personal. Allowing your partner insight into your world of literature is a romantic gift from one heart and mind to another.

- Ask your love about what he or she is reading.

- Many couples who have similar attitudes concerning art and culture, do not share the same taste in literature. Accept the fact that your partner may not want to read the book you have deemed a classic. He or she might, however, be interested in hearing the basis of your critique.

- Giving a gift of literature is risky business. After all, reading is a time commitment, and your spouse might feel obligated to read a book you have given, even if it isn't appealing. This can be prevented by asking for a book "wish list," or choosing from his or her favorite authors' work.

- Turn off the radio and television and sit quietly while reading along side your companion. Shared silence can be very relaxing and romantic.

- Read aloud to your partner while he or she works on another project. Later, you can discuss what you have read.

- Record your reading of an interesting magazine article, newspaper article, or short story, so your spouse can listen to it on a road trip or commute.

True Romance

A classic tale that is the very epitome of romance for Cheryl and I is O Henry's *Gift of the Magi*. This short story is about "Jim" and "Della" on the brink of Christmas who find that their meager finances make it impossible for them to exchange gifts. Their love is so great that the thought of not giving a well-deserved gift is unacceptable. The sacrifices they undergo to provide a joyous Christmas for each other speaks of that love; but the conclusion is breathtaking in its irony and, ultimately, in its display of love and hope. *The Gift of the Magi* sets the standard for romantic literature while providing a testament of the gifts that we all might share through love and romance. Together, we read this story at least every couple years, for it has profound meaning to us.

—Joe

Sealed With a Kiss

Love Letters

The love letter as a means of expression is without equal, allowing the writer time to get the message and tone just right. It permits editing opportunities absent in the spoken word. It inspires creative communication, and frees those who are uncomfortable expressing feelings. It can be lighthearted or profoundly personal. And somehow, the love letter makes the feelings of the writer official — right there in black and white — a lasting demonstration of love and devotion.

- Romantic gestures are often made up of small special touches. Visit your local stationery shop to find just the right medium for your message. Most well-stocked stores will have special paper or ink to match the subject or occasion you are writing about. Making the effort to add this small touch is a demonstration in itself of your caring.

- Before sitting down to write, give the subject some thought, so your feelings can be expressed in an articulate manner.

- The topic of a love letter can be varied. It can be general in nature, giving your partner the overall sense of his or her value in your life and in the lives of others. It may be specific, perhaps a thank you for a particular effort. The letter may provide reinforcement of your love or encouragement for challenges that lie ahead. In many cases, a motivating factor initiates the love letter, but a letter that communicates love, happiness, and respect is always in order.

- Carefully consider the salutation. It is really the first message of the letter and, as such, should be an open display of love and warmth, "For my special lady," "My beloved," "For my husband and ally."

- If a lack of literary skill is intimidating you, fear not. No one is going to grade your paper. The most important thing is that the message expresses your heartfelt feelings for your partner. Feel free to use your own speaking style. After all, the letter should sound like it is from you, not Shakespeare.

- If you perceive that you lack eloquence, rest assured that the person receiving your message will value it all the same. Your time and heartfelt thoughts are what make it meaningful.

- Be sure to date your love letter. These letters are frequently saved, becoming treasured heirlooms and time capsules of your relationship.

True Romance

Well this isn't really about a love letter, but it is about a love "message." Does that count? One morning I was running late, and I left for work in a hurry. I had no way of knowing that when I returned that evening, it would be to a burned-out shell of a home. We had had a house fire. Thankfully, no one had been hurt, but nevertheless it was a tremendous loss. As I walked through the wreckage to see if anything was left, I crossed by the bathroom and that's when I saw it. Written in soap on the bathroom mirror were the words, "I Love You." My wife had written that message for me after I had left for work, intending that I find it when I returned home. So there I stood in that sooty, wet, burned-out mess, having lost everything, staring at the only thing that seemed to have survived the fire — and that's when I realized that that was enough.

— Andy

Shop in the Name of Love

Gift-giving

In gift-giving, romantic opportunities abound. It is an area that exhibits some of the classic tenets of romance: the giving of time and the display of thoughtfulness. A hidden message is delivered with each gift — one more powerful than the gift itself — the sentiment involved. The right gift, properly presented and well timed, is strong evidence that the recipient is listened to, valued, and thought of, even when he or she is not present.

- The key is to give a gift that was obviously intended for just that person. Candy, perfume, gloves, neckties, and other common gifts can seem impersonal if not based on something you know about your partner. Find his or her favorite cologne. Buy a whole carton of the candy you know she can't resist. Order a sweatshirt sporting the logo of his favorite team.

- To maximize the enjoyment in receiving your gift, be sure it is wrapped. Write a few loving words on an accompanying card.

- Avoid buying gifts that are TOO practical. If your partner needs a new frying pan, vacuum cleaner, or long johns, try to purchase them from the household budget rather than on a special gift-giving occasion.

- When buying clothing, be sure you know the correct size. Refer to your handy-dandy laminated size information card that you carry with you, or check the tags on clothes in the closet if necessary. Buy the type of clothing your partner likes to wear, rather than what you would like them to wear.

- Gift-giving might be easier if you think of a "continuing" gift your partner would treasure. You might purchase pieces of gourmet cookware, china, or woodworking tools over time, which defers the high cost, and lets your spouse look forward to building a set, piece by piece. The same idea can be used in collecting prints by a favorite artist, albums from a favorite musician, or baseball cards of a favorite player or team.

- Coupons can be a fun way to give a meaningful gift. Personalized coupons might be handwritten or printed on a computer. With your own insights and creativity, the gift can be tailored to your partner's pleasures. When the coupon is redeemed, the recipient might be entitled to:
    - Back rub
    - Dinner at a favorite restaurant (or a special dinner cooked at home)
    - Movie date
    - Golfing or other favorite activity
    - Completion of a chore
    - Uninterrupted nap

- If your spouse is a major fan of a particular musical artist or band, he or she may already have a full collection of the band's records. Look for memorabilia related to the band, such as autographed photos, vintage touring posters, or 45-rpm picture sleeves. A framed album cover could also make an excellent gift for your "fanatic."

- Do a special house or yard project when your sweetheart is out of town. Put in a new flowerbed, or re-wallpaper a room as a surprise.

- Find a model of your spouse's favorite car, maybe the first car he or she owned.

- Give a gift of a trip. Rather than just giving the tickets, or saying, "We're going to Hawaii next month," give a few items that represent your destination — a beach towel, sunglasses, a travel book or poster. Or serve a meal appropriate to the culture when making the announcement of the trip.

- Personal photographs can be imprinted on a variety of items: mugs, shirts, mouse pads, paper weights, puzzles, etc. Use a photo that reminds you both of a happy time together.

- Have a nice portrait taken of yourself or you with the kids.

- Give the gift of a "test run" at whatever he or she always wanted to be. Pay for a visit to a dude ranch, sports camp, or arrange for him or her to drive a semi-truck or racecar.

- Make something yourself. With a few instructions, even a novice can make a simple birdhouse or photo collage. It will mean so much more than a similar item purchased from a store.

- Dedicate a song on the radio that will be played at a perfect moment.

- Hire a hot air balloon pilot, carriage driver, or limousine chauffeur to take the two of you on a romantic ride.

- Surround your gift with chocolate kisses to make even the packing material romantic.

True Romance

My husband was a "chewer." He chewed tobacco. I love him dearly, but that was a nasty habit. I wanted him to quit, but he said he enjoyed it too much to give it up. Five years ago on our anniversary, he gave me what felt like an empty can of tobacco. I opened it up to find a small piece of paper that read, "Keep this can as a family heirloom. It is the last can of tobacco I will ever chew. Happy Anniversary." True to his word, he never chewed again. What's more, the following anniversary he totaled up all the money he saved by ending his habit, and bought me a gift with the savings. I'm so proud of him. That empty tobacco can is the best gift I have ever received.

—Lynn

Kisses Sweeter Than Wine

The Kiss

One should not overlook the power of a kiss. In the early stages of a relationship, a kiss can seem almost intoxicating. In those days, the kiss seemed always in short supply (no matter the quantity) as they were limited by the time spent on a date. In long-term relationships, time and proximity to each other are much greater, but the kiss is not always accorded its due. But the fact of the matter is, just as in courtship, kissing remains the stuff of wonder.

- The stereotype of a kiss in married life is the "marriage peck." The peck can be upgraded to a kiss simply with an accompanying embrace and/or linger.

- If kissing skills are not maintained over time, they can erode. There is, however, no need to fear — the art of kissing can be regained. Of course, it may require practice...

- A tender kiss is a beautiful expression of love. Kissing should be considered a stand-alone enterprise, without expectation of what might follow. Enjoy the moment.

- Fresh breath and good dental hygiene will enhance the experience for both partners.

- As with dancing, one partner generally sets the kissing tempo. Unlike dancing, the lead can change from one partner to the other in mid-kiss. That's a good thing, and like any expression of love, should be encouraged.

- Although the subject is of some debate, kissing is in the lips.

- Always kissing hello and goodbye is a wonderful habit to get into. And remember, we're talking a kiss, not a marriage peck!

True Romance

Wow, your question is a tough one...I guess my most romantic memory is of a kiss. My then-boyfriend, now-husband, and I were attending a concert in our college days. It was an outdoor show with a fireworks display to follow. After the music ended, there was an intermission while the fireworks were set up. It was very dark and Rick took that opportunity to give me a long soft kiss. Just then, the fireworks went off with the most perfect timing imaginable. The silhouette of our kiss set the folks behind us to giggling. I think they could tell what I knew — that this was a kiss with staying power.

—**Pam**

Ticket to Ride

Travel

Beaches, parks, and other natural settings possess an air of romance, and are often associated with warm sentimental feelings. Man-made structures and facilities generally lack romantic attachment (with some notable exceptions). Transportation facilities such as seaports, airports, and train stations can be highly romantic. They are primarily places of utility, but they are also very personal. Though sometimes filled with sorrow and longing when loved ones are separated, they are places of overwhelming joy when lovers are reunited. And of course, travel stations represent hopefulness, where lovers embark on first and second honeymoons or on much-needed vacations.

Sometimes our most romantic experiences are away from home. Little getaways and long-planned vacations create special memories for years to come. Whether you travel to a tropical island or to a nearby campground, you will find new opportunities to set the stage for romance. Even when one partner must travel without the other, there are many ways to keep romance foremost in your minds.

•When your mate has to travel alone:

- See him or her off at the gate and be there upon return whenever possible.
- If it is a business trip, or a trip concerning a health or family situation, a note of encouragement and love will be appreciated.
- Enclose items to make the trip more comfortable such as hard candy, bottled water, crossword puzzles, and reading material.

•When you must travel alone:

- Leave a romantic note or card behind on your sweetheart's pillow.
- Arrange for a local flower shop to deliver your handpicked and signed card with flowers while you're away.
- Make, label, and freeze a meal or two so that all your partner has to do is reheat the dish. (This is appropriate whether or not you do most of the cooking.)
- If you primarily see to or perform the home and vehicle maintenance, prepare a phone list of competent local repairmen in the event that something fails or breaks while you are gone.
- Be sure to call or email regularly while you are away.
- Write a running letter during your days away — a journal of your activities to share with your partner when you return. Be sure to include feelings of love: "I am missing you so much. I wish you were here beside me!"

- An out-of-town vacation for the two of you is made for romance. It begins with the planning, especially when traveling to a new destination:
    - Research the area you plan to visit, and share the information with your spouse. The more you both know, the more excitement will be generated for the trip. Discuss together what you would most like to do with your time on vacation. Museums? Hiking? Relaxing by a pool? Often, couples find that the planning and anticipation is nearly as much fun as the trip itself.
    - Be sure to schedule in some time to relax and regroup. Recognize that traveling can be stressful; discuss this with your mate to prevent the dreaded "vacation fight."
    - Make a list of, and carry, provisions for long rides or layovers.
    - Take plenty of pictures and be sure to ask bystanders to take pictures of the two of you with your camera.
    - Bring back useful souvenirs from your trip together. Save paper items from the excursion, such as tickets and postcards for a trip scrapbook.
    - Although vacations always seem too short, tell each other that you are grateful for the time together.

- A semi-local vacation has merits too. The travel is less difficult and less time-consuming, which maximizes the prospects for relaxation and romance. A neighboring town might present rejuvenating getaway opportunities. Look for a bed and breakfast inn, secluded cabin, or elegant hotel for a special experience close to home. A nearby destination is also perfect for a, "Surprise! The car is already packed — let's go," weekend.

True Romance

One summer, when our boys were still quite young and I had been away on a business trip, my wife helped the kids hand paint a "Welcome Home" message on a large board and place it in the front yard for me to see when I returned. (Naturally, we took a picture of this, and although the sign was quite crude due to their ages, the photograph and the memory is one of our favorites to this day.)

—Barry

Celebrate Good Times

Holidays and Special Occasions

Everyone likes to have something to look forward to. Weekends, vacations, and parties provide the opportunity for fun and relaxation. Although holidays can require a good deal of work, they also offer great rewards, such as sharing time-honored traditions with close friends and family. Celebrations, whether large or small, bring merriment to our lives, and there is no need to wait for a red-letter date printed on the calendar.

- Couples often celebrate in the traditions learned and borrowed from their individual childhoods. These celebratory customs are very important, but it's never too late to establish your own traditions.

- Environment is important to the mood of any celebration, so decorate together — whether it's one room or the whole house.

- Observe a number of romantic anniversaries. Celebrate your first date, the day you got engaged, or the day you moved into your house.

- Write a holiday letter together and focus on positive events as you enjoy thinking back on the year.

- In late January, gather all the photos from the previous year. Reminisce while chronicling the preceding year by assembling a family photo album as a couple.

- To celebrate your wedding anniversary, re-experience your honeymoon. If you can't actually return to your original honeymoon locale, decorate and dress in a similar style, eat foods that you enjoyed on that special getaway, and listen to music from that year. A major anniversary might be a good time to renew your marriage proposal or vows.

- Always give yourselves something to look forward to. Celebrate a different religious, ethnic, or national holiday each month:
  - Throw a romantic New Year's party for two with your favorite dance music, hors d'oeuvres, champagne, and noisemakers. Make plans for the upcoming year together.
  - Whether you're a sports fan or not, watch the Super Bowl or World Series together on TV. The networks usually go all-out to appeal to even the most casual viewer. Make a pot of chili, "sub" sandwiches, or super nachos.
  - Valentine's Day was designed for lovers — make it a special occasion. Consider an unusual means for having a gift delivered. Ask the pizza parlor to make a heart-shaped pizza. You can easily make a heart-shaped cake with one square cake pan and one round. Cut the round cake in half, and place the cut edges on two adjoining sides of the square cake.

- Celebrate St. Patrick's Day by attending a parade, wearing green, and serving Irish stew or corn beef and cabbage. Have a bouquet of green balloons delivered.
- A traditional activity on May Day is to place a "May basket" of flowers on someone's doorstep, ring the bell, and run. Your love probably won't be expecting anything on May 1st, so give a card or have flowers delivered.
- Celebrate Cinco de Mayo with a meal of chili rellenos, tamale pie, tortillas, rice, beans, and margaritas.
- Give your wife the day off on Mother's Day, or develop your own interesting way to celebrate this special day.
- Have fun with your husband on Father's Day. Let the kids romp in a creek while you and your husband spoon under a tree.
- Be festive during Summer Solstice. Drink lemonade, listen to the Beach Boys, take in a baseball game.
- Plan your own patriotic Fourth-of-July party with flags, picnic foods, and fireworks. Read the Declaration of Independence together.
- Celebrate the working class on Labor Day. Use this day to do fall chores together in the yard, then admire the accomplishments of good old-fashioned manual labor.
- Carve a pumpkin together and roast the seeds. Make a face like the finished jack-o-lantern, and take a memorable picture.
- Together, call to thank a veteran on Veteran's Day for having served our country.
- As the holidays approach, think charitably! As a couple, help distribute food to the poor.
- Discuss Thanksgiving plans well in advance. Decide on a menu, guests, division of labor and, if applicable, travel plans. If you are hosting the meal, prepare as many dishes as possible ahead, to reduce stress on Thanksgiving Day. Most importantly, give thanks and feast!
- Go see "The Nutcracker" ballet during the holidays and take an evening drive to look at Christmas lights.
- On Christmas, express your thankfulness for the blessings of the year. Take time to sit in the glow of the Christmas tree lights together. Read a treasured holiday story. To relax after dinner, watch videos of past family Christmases or play a new board game together.

True Romance

My widowed grandmother remarried when she was in her 80s. She and her husband, thinking they might not have very many anniversaries to share, celebrate "monthaversaries."

—Jane

We Can Work It Out

Tiffs

Conflicts exist in all relationships. Constructive criticism and disagreements, though not pleasant, are necessary in a healthy marriage. Through conflict and its eventual resolution, relationships have a much-needed "pressure-release valve" that allows issues to be confronted and discussed in a caring environment. If both parties set self-interest aside and bring forth points and ideas with love and respect, while thoughtfully listening to the other's response, resolution can come quickly. Neither partner needs to feel like a "winner" or "loser" if you are working together to solve a mutual concern. Most couples would agree that challenges in general, and challenges within the relationship, are best met as a team.

- Listening cannot be overemphasized. In many instances, couples find that after several minutes of heated discussion, they are not even arguing about the same issue, but rather some variation on a general theme.

- Frequently, the cause of a disagreement is stress outside the marriage that manifests itself in the relationship. Be sensitive to what might be underlying the tension.

- During a quarrel, choose your words carefully. The subject of most arguments is forgotten long before the hurtful messages that erupt from them.

- Be mindful of your body language. No cause was ever served by slamming anything.

- The scope of a conflict both enlarges and blurs if one partner walks out during a dispute.

- During a disagreement, it is not helpful to air a "laundry list" of past offenses. Stay on the subject at hand and work through it.

- Sometimes during the course of an argument, feelings are minimized or trivialized through misunderstanding. If you aren't readily able to see your partner's point of view or understand the basis of his or her feelings, say so in a simple direct manner without implication.

- On occasion, a difference of opinion escalates at a rapid pace. Interrupt that pace by stopping to reiterate that despite the heat of the moment, you love and respect your spouse and do not wish to hurt his or her feelings.

- The silent treatment is a completely ineffective tactic in problem resolution.

- It is as important to learn to accept your mate's apologies, as it is to say you're sorry.

- To truly put a disagreement to rest, both parties must forgive and forget. Take the lead on this one.

- The wisdom of the old adages that couples should not go to bed mad or leave the house angry cannot be argued.

True Romance

One thing I appreciate about my husband is that when I am upset, he always takes time to talk it out with me. Sometimes he has been late for work, or we have missed a social engagement because he wanted to make sure we were OK.

—Susan

I'm a Believer

Faith Matters

Spiritual matters are deeply personal and each relationship with God is unique and individual. For some, these feelings are so personal that the topic is off limits for discussion altogether. Others will freely share their beliefs. Obviously, there is a lot of middle ground. The approach to matters of faith within the marriage is widely varied as well. Some couples have a strong relationship with God while others have no relationship at all. Some couples attend church services regularly, some not at all. Some couples discuss faith easily; others are reluctant to broach the subject. One thing that is certain is that faith and church service attendance are perhaps the greatest resources available to the couple in terms of strengthening, counseling, and reassurance. It stems from a message that has been consistent and unwavering through the ages. A message that remains untouched by cultural change or faddish phenomena. A message that speaks of love, forgiveness, and mercy. A message that addresses the sanctity of marriage and the trials of life. A message of service, compassion, and ultimately hope and renewal. The very foundation of a successful marriage may be found in the word of God.

- If you feel comfortable praying aloud with your partner, do so. It will be inspirational to hear you pray on his or her behalf, or in thankfulness for your many blessings.

- Discussing the message of a service or of religious reading material allows for increased understanding through the sharing of perspectives. This also aids intellectual and spiritual growth.

- A byproduct of attending religious services is the opportunity to meet people with similar values, making the church a place where new friendships are formed.

- Everyone starts somewhere in his or her acquisition of spiritual knowledge and beliefs. The two of you don't need to know a thing to get started in this endeavor, and you need not come from similar religious backgrounds. As you have done with all that came before, take this journey together. It is a pathway resplendent in rewards.

True Romance

Before we were married, my husband agreed he would go to church with me, even though it was not something he really wanted to do. Later, I felt like it was a chore to get him to go. He went, but very reluctantly. Together, we sought a church where we could both feel comfortable. It was a joy to watch him grow to actually enjoy going! Now, our church experience has become a very special part of both our lives.

—Bonnie

Learning to Fly

Intellectual Growth

It doesn't happen by itself. In order to increase, or even maintain, intellectual skills in such areas as reasoning, comprehension, and judgment, the mind must be ever stimulated. Regular mental enhancement can benefit a relationship as well. Couples that set upon a life's journey of intellectual growth are rewarded with enriched conversation, improved problem solving abilities, and general enlightenment.

- Whether it is a magazine article or a multi-volume historical biography, share and discuss interesting information with the one you love.

- Take a class or attend a workshop together. So many options are available that there is sure to be something for every couple. In rural areas, correspondence courses might be an alternative. Some classes seem tailored for romance, such as dance classes and marriage encounter sessions.

- On your own, take a class to learn skills that you can apply to a romantic undertaking. In an art or carpentry class, you might learn to construct a handmade gift. Or attend a tile or wall-papering workshop for a surprise remodeling job.

- Even if you are proficient at a favorite activity, taking lessons can increase your skills and your enjoyment.

- Perhaps the greatest teacher of all is life. Learn from what you have done right, and from what you have done wrong. Discuss these life lessons with your special someone; his or her trusted perspective is invaluable.

True Romance

My wife and I like to discuss articles from the newspaper. It is one way we can learn more about each other and even learn from each other.

—Les

Some Assembly Required

Hobbies

A person's chosen hobby speaks much of the individual. It is often a component of personality that does not have an outlet in day-to-day life. A hobby is a form of escapism and relaxation. In married life, hobbies are often set aside in favor of other important interests. Feelings of guilt might be associated with pursuing hobbies, as it generally takes time from the family. That need not be the case. Because hobbies enrich and relax those who are undertaking them, they should be encouraged, and with a little creativity, the heretofore individual hobby can be enjoyed by two.

- Look for ways to mesh your two existing hobbies or undertake a new one for yourself. Curl up with a book or crossword puzzle beside your mate while he or she surfs the Internet or watches TV. Listen to music while the other sews or ties flies for fishing. If camping or hunting is your partner's thing, try taking up a hobby that allows you to go along, such as photography, bird watching, or flora identification. Proximity allows for sharing.

- No one needs to be a golf or tennis widow or widower. Take lessons from a club pro, then join your partner in enjoying his or her favorite activity.

- Help your spouse rekindle an interest in an old hobby.

- Almost everyone likes to talk about his or her hobbies. Show support by asking questions. Find out how your partner was introduced to the hobby and why he or she enjoys it. Learn enough about it to understand the "lingo."

- Attend a hobby show or convention together. These events can sometimes be worked into a surprise weekend getaway for the two of you.

- Establishing a new shared hobby is rewarding. Try a few things until you hit on something that you both enjoy, such as gardening, genealogy research, exercising, fishing, learning a foreign language, or working on home improvements projects together.

- If your spouse has kindly afforded you free time to pursue a favorite activity, appreciatively take that time for you to enjoy yourself.

True Romance

Metal detecting is my husband's hobby. Now, I have no real interest in metal detecting, but he and I like being together, so we've tried to create ways to spend time near each other, even if we are not interacting. This summer, we decided to combine his metal detecting and my exercising routine. We chose the old high school football grounds, where he looks for treasures while I do my walking around the track. Every couple of trips around, I check in with him to see what he's found.

—Karen

An Eye on the Prize

Goal Setting

It's the mantra of Business 101: Planning is the foundation of all successful business enterprises. The concept applies to romantic endeavors as well. Couples continually make short-term plans to navigate their way through daily life. Long-term planning and goal-setting sessions are less frequently undertaken, but are of great value in a relationship. Discussions involving long-term goals bring a tremendously unifying force to a relationship.

- Who better to plan with than your mate? In an atmosphere where ideas and dreams may be freely expressed, much can be accomplished.

- Any forum for discussion will do, whether lounging together on a Sunday afternoon or sitting with pad and pencil at the kitchen table. No matter the setting, joint planning will help keep the couple's future on the same page.

- Actual planning discussions may be a casual exchange of ideas or be more structured. For those couples favoring structure, that approach may take several different forms. The couples might list goals by what they must accomplish, then by what they would like to accomplish, and finally what they might wish to accomplish under the best-case scenario. This approach is useful, illuminating, and fun.

- Be sure that your spouse's goals receive at least equal time in planning.

- Include a discussion on how your objectives might be accomplished. You might pencil in a timeline, but maintain realistic expectations to avoid future disappointments.

- Because life is uncertain, couples should be flexible in their planning, and update goals periodically.

- The most important aspect of the process is to plan together in the present to serve the best interest of the couple for the future. That is pure romance.

True Romance

We are "list people." My husband and I write down the things we have to do in daily planner books. It is our way of keeping our sanity and not forgetting or being late for an appointment or something. We are goal setters, as well, and we keep lists for that too. The great thing about goal-setting lists, (which for us tend to be more long-term, usually seasonal), is that after we finish a task, we get to cross it off the list. Sometimes we forget how much we have accomplished as a team, but when, for instance, we retire the "spring list" and begin the "summer list," the proof is right there. We really do get a lot of things done.

—Terrie

Now and Forever

The Wrap-up

The strength and depth of a longstanding, loving relationship is something to behold. Like all great wonders, it is not created in an instant. Instead, it is formed and sculpted over time through a variety of influences. It is certain that no influence has a more positive and profound effect on the relationship than romance: a partner's willing practice of service, sacrifice, and thoughtfulness for his or her loved one. These acts serve as testament to the respect, value, and joy of the relationship. There is simply no better way to say I love you...now and forever.

Acknowledgments

Joe and Cheryl wish to thank the following:

Carol Jane Seidlitz
Arleen Darling
Sheila Homme
Edward Homme

And to all of you who shared your *True Romance* stories with us, we sincerely thank you for participating in this project.

Grow old along with me,
The best is yet to be.

—Robert Browning